BEAR AWARE

Hiking and Camping in Bear Country

Bill Schneider

FALCON™

Helena, Montana

Editing, design, typesetting and other pre-press work by Falcon Press,
Helena, Montana. Printed in Canada.

ISBN 1-56044-456-8

CAUTION

Outdoor recreation can be dangerous, including hiking and
camping in bear country. Everybody who goes into bear country
assumes some risk and responsibility for his or her own actions
and safety.

The information contained in this book is a summary of the
author's personal experiences, review of existing literature on bear-
human encounters, and conversations with numerous bear experts.
The book has been reviewed by bear experts prior to publication.
However, neither this book (nor any other book) can assure your
safety from bears. Neither this book, nor any other book, can
replace sound judgment and good decision-making skills, which
will greatly reduce the risks of going into bear country. The scope
of this book does not allow for disclosure of all the potential haz-
ards and risks of going into bear country.

Learn as much as possible from this book and other sources of
information, and prepare for the unexpected. Be safe and cautious.
The reward will be a safer and more enjoyable experience.

Dear Bill,

You'd be proud of me. I did it. I just finished a five-day backpacking trip in Yellowstone. And I didn't see a single grizzly, but at night in my tent I heard hundreds of them.

Your friend, Pat

Acknowledgments

This book is much more than the work of one author. Through the years, I have spent many hours discussing this subject with peer researchers, wildlife managers, park rangers, and leaders of environmental groups. Actually, the number of people who really contributed to this book would be too numerous to list.

However, I do want to thank Kerry Gunther from the National Park Service in Yellowstone National Park, Tom Puchlerz from the Northern Region of the USDA Forest Service, Chris Servheen from the U.S. Fish and Wildlife Service's Interagency Grizzly Bear Team, Chuck Bartlebaugh from the Center for Wildlife Information, and Chuck Jonkel, a bear scientist, for their thorough review of the draft manuscript.

Again, they would be too numerous to name, but the impetus for this book and many of the questions it answers came from the hundreds of people who attended my classes on hiking and camping in grizzly country taught for twelve years at the Yellowstone Institute.

I also want to thank the illustrator, Kirk Botero, and the staff of Falcon Press Publishing Company for doing such a superb job on the book.

Contents

Two Sides to Every Story

We are apprehensive that as more people make use of the bears' shrinking domain, an increase in bear attacks or maulings might precipitate a reaction that could result in wholesale destruction of the animals.—Dr. Frank C. Craighead, Jr.

Statistically, you're quite safe from bears. Following the guidelines in this book reduces the likelihood of you becoming a statistic even more. Bears definitely add an additional risk to your trip, but you take a much greater risk driving to the trailhead. And even if you do die on your hike, you're much more likely to drown, fall off a cliff, suffer heart failure or other sudden illness, or succumb to hypothermia.

Auto accidents, some very grisly, claim thousands of lives every year, but these news stories get buried deep within the daily newspaper. However, a bear mauling commands front-page headlines, and we read every word, right? This phenomenon won't change, but we must be careful to keep the danger posed by bears in perspective.

Domestic dogs kill more people than bears. So do bees, Hereford bulls, and lightning. Walking the streets of Washington, D.C., or Detroit is much more hazardous than walking in bear country. Central Park is more dangerous than Yellowstone Park.

Yes, bears have caused human injury or death. Hopefully, however, with the distribution of more information on how to safely hike and camp in bear country, fewer and fewer bears will make the front page and more and more people can safely enjoy the wilderness.

That's our side of the story. There's also the other side, the bear's side.

Carelessness can kill not only you and me, but also the bear. Sometimes the aftermath of a bear mauling is a dead bear.

In many cases, such as a sudden encounter where a female is protecting her cubs, rangers and wildlife managers take no action against the bear. However, in cases where the bear has lost its fear of humankind, rangers have little choice but to designate the bear a dangerous offender and kill it. In other cases, arguably worse, they take the bear from the wild and banish it for life in a research lab, zoo, or drive-through wildlife park.

In other cases, the bear gradually becomes more habituated to human food or garbage. Once a bear picks up this bad habit, it's a slow, but virtually guaranteed, death. The bear might stave off its fate for years, but in the end it crosses over the line, and authorities "remove it from the population."

Females with cubs often range in low-lying areas along streams. Our roads and developments often occur in the same places. This often exposes females with cubs to human encounters or gives them access to human food or garbage. Reproducing females are, by far, the most critical element of a bear population, and the loss of just a few can threaten the existence of the entire population. Plus, females pass on behavioral traits to the cubs, and they can pass along terminal habits such as feeding on garbage or experience gained during an encounter with a hiker.

Obviously, bear encounters pose a threat to human safety. However, these encounters also pose a threat to bear safety—and not just individual bears, but the entire population.

This side of the story doesn't make many headlines. However, it's another reason we should take every possible precaution to avoid an encounter. Too many bear encounters could even lead to a movement to rid the forests of bears.

Therefore, there are two reasons for this book. This book can save you, but it can save a bear, too.

Bear Sense

Your best weapon to minimize the risk of a bear attack is your brain. Use it as soon as you contemplate a trip to bear country, and continue to use it throughout your stay.

—Dr. Stephen Herrero

DON'T GENERALIZE

One reason it's difficult to separate fact from fiction is because bears have a way of proving the experts wrong. As soon as somebody says "bears never do this," a bear comes along and does it. So be wary of any absolute statement about bears.

BE BEAR AWARE

Knowledge is the best defense. Hikers who know about bears have already taken the vital first step.

Knowledgeable hikers know what kind of equipment to bring, how to set up camp, when and where to be most careful, and what bear and human behavior increases the chance of a bear attack. Since every bear encounter is different, informed hikers can also much more easily improvise and deal with every situation.

Here are the answers to a few of the most commonly asked questions about bears.

IS THERE ANY WAY TO BE ABSOLUTELY SAFE?

No. There is no way to guarantee total safety while hiking and camping in bear country. However, you can greatly minimize the risk of being injured.

WHAT'S THE DIFFERENCE BETWEEN BLACK BEARS AND GRIZZLY BEARS?

Black and grizzly bears differ significantly. From one important perspective, however, there is no difference. Both species are dangerous. One common —and serious—mistake is thinking that

only grizzlies are dangerous. All bears are dangerous and should be treated as one dangerous species.

A typical bear is as mythical as a typical person.

In fact, black bears cause more injuries than
grizzly bears, but grizzlies cause more serious injuries and fatalities. This is largely due to the fact
that North America has many more black bears in
many more places, but it's partly due to a noncha-
lant attitude toward black bears. Never view a black
bear as "Yogi" or "Smokey." Instead, view black
bears as dangerous wild animals, just like grizzlies.

Black bears and grizzlies commonly occur in
the same habitat and sometimes identification can
be difficult. This is another reason to treat all bears
as one dangerous species. That blackish-colored
bear could be a grizzly.

Even though identification of certain bears can
be difficult, the two species differ in many ways.
See the graphics on pages 14-17.

GRIZZLY BEAR

Ursus horribilis

Color: Black to blond, frequently silver-tipped, giving a grizzled appearance.

Size: About 3-4 feet tall at shoulder, often over 6-8 feet tall when standing, 200 to 700 pounds in interior areas, and up to 1,200 pounds in coastal areas.

Distinguishing features: Prominent hump over shoulders, sloping back line, dished or concave face, large head, long curved claws that are usually light-colored and rarely less than 1.75 inches long.

BLACK BEAR

Ursus americanus

Color: Black to blond, but usually with a muzzle that's a lighter color than the body, often with a white patch on throat or chest.

Size: About 2-3 feet tall at shoulder, about 4-5 feet tall when standing, 150 to 500 pounds.

Distinguishing features: Small size, straight facial profile, straight back line, small head, shorter claws that are usually dark-colored and rarely more than 1.5 inches long.

BLACK BEAR

GRIZZLY BEAR

NOTE: Even bear experts have a hard time distinguishing between a small grizzly and a large black bear. Size and color cannot be used to identify bears. Treat all bears as dangerous wild animals.

BLACK BEAR   **GRIZZLY BEAR**

BLACK BEAR RANGE

GRIZZLY BEAR RANGE

DO BEARS STAY IN THE SAME PLACE
OR DO THEY MOVE AROUND?

Both. Some bears stay close to a specific habitat while others will range widely, as much as 50 miles per day.

Habitat, reproductive status, and food supply usually dictate bear movement. Bears usually stay close to a good food source such as a carcass or berry patch. In the spring, when much of the high country remains carpeted with snow, bears often hang around stream bottoms feeding on emerging vegetation. In late summer and fall, they move to berry patches and groves of whitebark pines. Never assume "there aren't any bears around here," and keep in mind that you can find bears anywhere in their range.

WHAT DO BEARS EAT?

Almost anything. Bears are technically called carnivores, but they are primarily vegetarians and would best be called omnivores. They might also be called opportunists, since they almost always go for the easiest available meal, meat or vegetable.

Along the salmon streams of Alaska and Canada, bears commonly feast on the rich food supply provided by spawning salmon. But in most inland areas, bears feed primarily on foliage, roots, insects, nuts, and berries. Some studies have found that more than 90 percent of a bear's diet is vegetative matter. In other words, you're much more likely to see a bear grazing like an elk than chasing an elk down for dinner.

> A leaf fell in the woods.
> The eagle saw it.
> The deer heard it.
> And the bear smelled it.

HOW DO BEARS KNOW WHERE YOU ARE?

Bears primarily use their sense of smell to detect

danger or food. However, they also have an excellent sense of hearing. Bears have better vision than commonly believed, but they do not use their eyes nearly as much as their nose or ears.

WHY DON'T BEARS JUST STAY AWAY FROM PEOPLE?

They try to, but they can't. There are virtually no places left just for bears. More and more hikers forge deeper and deeper into the remotest country, so bears just can't stay away from us or our camps, temporary or permanent.

HOW DO YOU KNOW IF THERE ARE BEARS AROUND?

Sometimes you can, but sometimes you can't. Bears leave signs, of course, such as scats, tracks, diggings, and bark ripped off trees. Try to familiarize yourself with these signs before hiking in bear country. However, bears are secretive and wide-ranging, and just because you haven't seen any sign, don't assume there are no bears around.

HOW DANGEROUS ARE BEARS?

All bears should be viewed as dangerous, but statistically, they are not really very dangerous—at least compared to other threats to human life. Actually, statistics can also be dangerous. Be careful not to rely on them too much, since the numbers can give you false confidence that might prompt you to skip some of the precautions recommended later in this book. Also, many statistics are only the best estimates of bear experts.

North America probably has 500,000 to 600,000 bears, mostly black bears. Yet, to date, fewer than 50 people have been killed by bears. For each recorded fatality caused by bears (all species), there are approximately 8 caused by spiders, 13 by snakes, 34 by domestic dogs, 90 by bees and wasps, and 190 by lightning.

There are about 50 black bears for every grizzly bear in North America, but each species is responsible for approximately one-half of the total fatalities traced to bears. This, of course, makes grizzly bears much more dangerous than black bears. Yet, even national parks with viable grizzly bear populations average fewer than one fatality per year—and millions of people visit these national parks every year.

Bear Mythology: Have You Heard This One?

But is the grizzly bear ferocious? All the first-hand evidence I can find says he is not. Speaking from years of experience with him my answer is emphatically, No!

During the greatest part of my life, I have lived in a grizzly bear region. I have camped for months alone and without a gun in their territory. I have seen them when alone and when with hunters. In Colorado, Utah, Arizona, Mexico, Wyoming, Montana, Idaho, Washington,

British Columbia and Alaska, I have spent weeks trailing and watching grizzlies, and their tracks in the snow showed that they trailed me.

They frequently came close, and there were times when they might have attacked me with every advantage. But they did not do so. As they never made any attack on me, nor on anyone else that I know of who was not bent on killing them, I can only conclude that they are not ferocious.—Enos Mills

People die. Bears die. But some of the old myths about bears never seem to die. Unfortunately, some myths about bears have persisted so long that they seem like fact when they are either pure fiction or definitely do not equal reality. Here are a few examples.

BEARS ARE SLOW

Reality check. Bears sometimes look slow, but that's as far from the truth as you can get. Bears can sprint 35-40 miles per hour for a short distance, faster than a racehorse and fast enough to run down an elk or deer—and about twice as fast as the fastest human being.

BEARS CAN'T RUN DOWNHILL

Reality check. Bears can run extremely fast uphill and downhill. Just because bears have shorter front legs than hind legs certainly doesn't mean they have trouble running in any terrain.

BEARS CAN'T CLIMB TREES

Reality check. Actually, mature grizzly bears can climb almost any tree (even trees with branch-free trunks), but they are rarely motivated to do so, probably because it's difficult to do. If you can easily climb the tree, then the mature grizzly bear probably can, too. Also, keep in mind that grizzlies can reach 10 feet up a tree. All black bears can proficiently climb trees—and frequently do.

BEARS CAN'T SEE

Reality check. As near as scientists can determine, bears can see about as well as humans can. One theory states that bears commonly see better when young and suffer from failing vision in old age. Sound familiar? Also, some scientists believe that bears might be color blind.

BEARS ARE AFRAID OF DOGS

Reality check. Some dogs chase bears, but these dogs are rarely "man's best friend" lying around the house most of the year waiting for those one or two weeks when they can come along to "protect" you on your planned backpacking vacation.

More commonly, bears chase or kill dogs, an excellent reason not to bring Fido on your wilderness trek. Your dog might run across a bear and the bear could chase your "best friend" back to its master, and then, of course, you would have a big problem. Any dog in bear country must be carefully controlled and not allowed to run free.

BLACK BEARS AREN'T DANGEROUS

Reality check. All bears are dangerous, but statistically black bears may be more dangerous than grizzly bears. Black bears have injured more people than grizzlies have, and black bears occur in more areas than grizzlies do, increasing your chances of encountering a bear.

BEARS AREN'T AROUND
DEVELOPED AREAS

Reality check. You might find more bears around developed areas than you would in the remote backcountry. Bears can be very secretive. Just because you or your friends haven't seen bears around a developed area doesn't mean they aren't there.

Keep in mind that humans gravitate to the

same high-quality habitat as bears do. We put our settlements along streams, in low country with rich soils and diverse vegetation. Bears and humans like the same places.

In addition, some people are still careless with garbage, allowing bears to feed on it. In some tourism developments, proprietors of hotels and restaurants actually feed bears on purpose to attract bear-watching tourists. These circumstances could make hiking in close proximity to developed areas more dangerous than hiking 10 miles from the nearest road.

BEARS DON'T USE TRAILS

Reality check. Bears frequently use trails because they offer the path of least resistance. You would not fight through thick underbrush when you could use a well-maintained trail, so why would a bear?

BEARS ONLY COME OUT AT NIGHT

Reality check. Bears are usually more active around dusk and dawn, and sometimes they remain active during the day, especially on cool, wet days or during the early spring or late fall. They can also be active throughout the night. This means you have at least a small chance of seeing a bear at any time of the day or night. Nonetheless, hiking at night is especially dangerous.

BEARS CAN'T SWIM

Reality check. Bears love water and are excellent swimmers.

HORSES ATTRACT BEARS

Reality check. Nobody knows for sure if horses attract or deter bears (or neither), but horses normally make more noise on the trail than hikers. Horses also sense bears before we do, so it's more likely that horses are a deterrent.

There is not a single recorded incident of a backcountry traveler being mauled by a bear while riding a horse. However, a few people have been hurt after being thrown from a horse spooked by a bear.

SMOKE FROM CAMPFIRES
ATTRACTS BEARS

Reality check. There is no scientific evidence to support this, nor have there been any encounters linked to campfire smoke. It's just as likely that campfire smoke serves as a deterrent by alerting bears for miles around of your presence. However, cooking over a campfire (as opposed to a back-packing stove) could more widely disperse food odors and, perhaps, attract bears.

Hiking in Bear Country

Are grizzly bears killers? I would have to say no. If the grizzly bear were half as bad as commonly portrayed, early explorers and frontiersmen would not have gotten far across the prairies, and the opening of the West would likely have been delayed until the advent of the repeating rifle. —ANDY RUSSELL

The first step of any hike in bear country is an attitude adjustment. Nothing guarantees total safety. Hiking in bear country adds a small risk to your trip. However, that risk can be greatly minimized by adhering to this age-old piece of advice—be prepared. And being prepared doesn't

only mean having the right equipment. It also means having the right knowledge.

Knowledge is the best defense.

DON'T LET FEAR RUIN YOUR TRIP

You can—and should—thoroughly enjoy your trip to bear country. Don't let the fear of bears ruin your vacation. This fear can accompany you every step of the way. It can constantly lurk in the back of your mind, preventing you from enjoying the wildest and most beautiful places left on earth. And even worse, some bear experts think bears might actually be able to sense your fear.

Being prepared and knowledgeable gives you confidence. It allows you to fight back the fear that can burden you throughout your stay in bear country. You won't—nor should you—forget about bears and the basic rules of safety, but proper preparation allows you to keep the fear of bears at bay and let enjoyment rule the day.

Defensive driving works. So does defensive hiking.

DO WE REALLY WANT TO BE TOTALLY SAFE?

If we really wanted to be totally safe, we probably would never go hiking in the wilderness—bears or no bears. We certainly wouldn't, at much greater risk, drive hundreds of miles to get to the trailhead. Perhaps a tinge of danger adds a desired element to our wilderness trip.

THE FIVE BASIC RULES OF HIKING SAFELY

Nobody likes surprises, and bears dislike them, too. The majority of bear maulings occur when a hiker surprises a bear. Therefore, it's vital to do everything possible to avoid these surprise meetings. Perhaps the best way is to know the five-part system that could be called "The Basic Five."

1. Be alert.
2. Go in a large group and stay together.
3. Stay on the trail.
4. Hike in the middle of the day.
5. Make metallic noise.

If you follow these five rules, the chance of encountering a bear on the trail sinks to the slimmest possible margin.

NO SUBSTITUTE FOR ALERTNESS

As you hike, watch ahead and to the sides. Don't fall into the all-too-common and particularly nasty habit of fixating on the trail 10 feet ahead. It's especially easy to do this when dragging a heavy pack up a long hill or when carefully watching your step on a heavily eroded trail.

Using your knowledge of bear habitat and habits, be especially alert in areas most likely to be frequented by bears such as avalanche chutes, berry patches, along streams, through stands of whitebark pine, etc.

Watch carefully for bear sign and be especially watchful (and noisy) if you see any. If you see a track or a scat but it doesn't look fresh, pretend it's fresh. This area is obviously frequented by bears.

WATCH THE WIND

The wind can be a friend or foe. The strength and direction of the wind can make a significant difference in your chances of an encounter with a bear.

When the wind is blowing at your back, you are much safer, since your smell is traveling ahead of you, alerting any bear that might be on or near the trail ahead. Conversely, when the wind is blowing in your face, your chances of a surprise meeting with a bear increase, so make more noise and be more alert.

A strong wind can also be noisy and limit a bear's ability to hear you coming. If a bear can't smell or hear you coming, the chances of an encounter greatly increase, so be aware of the wind.

IT'S TRUE. THERE IS SAFETY IN NUMBERS.

There have been very few instances where a large group has had a serious encounter with a bear. On the other hand, a large percentage of hikers mauled by bears were hiking alone. Large groups naturally make more noise and put out more smell and probably appear more threatening to bears. In addition, if you're hiking alone and get injured, there is nobody to go for help. For these reasons, some national parks recommend parties of four or more hikers when going into bear country.

If the large party splits up, it becomes two or more small parties, and the advantage is lost. So stay together. If you're on a family hike, keep the kids from running ahead. If you're in a large group, keep the stronger members from going ahead or weaker members from lagging behind. The best way to prevent this natural separation is to ask one of the slowest members of the group to lead. This keeps everybody together.

PEOPLE ARE SUPPOSED TO BE ON TRAILS

Although bears use trails, they don't often use them during midday when hikers commonly use them. Through generations of associating trails with people, bears probably expect to find hikers on trails, especially during midday.

Contrarily, bears probably don't expect to find hikers off trails. Bears rarely settle down in a day bed right along a heavily used trail. However, if you wander around in thickets off the trail (where bears probably don't expect to find hikers), you might stumble into an occupied day bed or cross paths with a traveling bear.

SLEEPING LATE
CAN HAVE ITS ADVANTAGES

Bears—and most other wildlife—usually aren't active during the middle of a day, especially on a hot summer day. Wild animals are most active around dawn and dusk. Therefore, hiking early in the morning or late afternoon increases your chances of seeing wildlife, including bears. Likewise, hiking from 11 a.m. to 3 p.m. on a hot August day greatly reduces the chance of an encounter.

SOME SOUNDS ARE BETTER THAN OTHERS

Perhaps the best way to avoid a surprise meeting with a bear is to make sure the bear knows you're coming, so make lots of noise. Metallic noise is vastly superior to human voices, which can be muffled by natural conditions. Even clapping or yelling loudly is not as effective as metallic noise such as bear bells, pebbles rattling in a can, an aluminum rod case, or metal-tipped walking stick clanging on rocks.

Before hitting the trail, your group might form a pact to keep up a constant stream of conversation, to sing, to tell jokes, and to make other noise. But be careful. At some inopportune point, concentration might slip and quiet could befall the crowd.

Most people would be amazed how fast a forest can absorb human voices. You can test this by going a hundred yards over a small hill or around a curve in the trail and see if you can hear your friends talking. In addition, natural conditions such as strong wind, an afternoon thundershower, or loud, rushing mountain streams can virtually erase the sound of human voices.

Metallic noise carries farther and most important, it could never simulate any natural sound. Even loud whistles can roughly simulate natural sounds such as marmot whistles and bird calls. But the sound of metal striking metal never occurs in nature.

The downside of metallic noise is that you probably hate it. You probably went hiking to get away from it, and the constant ringing of a bear bell can be most aggravating. Nonetheless, if you want to be as safe as possible, get out the bell or a can of pebbles and attach it to your belt or pack. You can also get bells to tie onto your shoelaces. These methods assure a constant ringing whenever you're moving.

Another noise proven to deter bears is an air horn. This works especially well in areas obviously frequented by bears, when you want to be very sure they know you are coming through. You can get portable air horns at marine supply shops.

And, of course, don't leave home unprepared. Make sure you bring some noise-making device along with you.

YOU DON'T NEED A BETTER VIEW

If you see a bear, don't try to get closer for a better look. The bear might interpret this as an act of aggression and charge.

GET A LONGER LENS INSTEAD

An unusually high percentage of people mauled by bears are photographers. That's because they are purposely being quiet hoping to see wildlife. In some cases, they see a bear and try to get closer for a better photo. Such behavior is counter to all rules of safety for hiking in bear country.

NOT ALWAYS MAN'S BEST FRIEND

Although many people relish the idea of taking

their faithful dog along on hikes, most experts
believe this is dangerous. In several documented
cases, dogs have attracted bears back to their own-
ers and the result has been a serious injury. Only
specially trained dogs can protect you from bears.
And besides, most national parks prohibit taking
pets on backcountry trails.

RUNNING UP THE RISK FACTOR

Many avid runners like to get off paved roads and
running tracks and onto backcountry trails. But
running on trails in bear country can be seriously
hazardous to your health.

Most runners avoid running during the heat
of the day. This means they run early or late in the
day when bears are most active.

Runners rarely make enough noise when running, and they might even sound like a wild animal
(i.e., prey for bears) running on a trail. Fervent
trail runners know that you tend to get closer to
wildlife running than you do walking. Some people

think that's because you cover distance faster than expected by wildlife. Other people think it's because you tend to be quieter when running. Whatever the reason, running on trails obviously increases your chance of surprising a bear.

The best advice is to avoid running in bear country, but if you're a hopelessly addicted runner and can't resist trying a scenic trail in bear country, at least strap a bell on your fanny pack.

LEAVE THE NIGHT TO THE BEARS

Like running on trails, hiking at night can be very risky. Bears are more active after dark, and you can't see them until it's too late. If you get caught out at night, be sure to make lots of metallic noise.

YOU CAN BE DEAD MEAT, TOO

If you see or smell a carcass of a dead animal when hiking, immediately vacate the area. Don't let your curiosity keep you near the carcass a second longer than you need to recognize this as a very dangerous situation.

Bears commonly hang around a carcass, guarding it and feeding on it for days until it's completely consumed. Your presence easily could be interpreted as a threat to the bear's food supply, and a vicious attack could be imminent.

If you see a carcass ahead of you on the trail, don't go any closer. Instead, abandon your hike and return to the trailhead. If the carcass is between you and the trailhead, take a very long detour around it, upwind from the carcass, making lots of noise along the way. Be sure to report the carcass to the local ranger or game warden. This might prompt a temporary trail closure or special warnings and prevent injury to other hikers. Rangers will, in some cases, go in and drag the carcass away from the trail.

CUTE, CUDDLY, AND LETHAL

The same goes for bear cubs. If you see one, don't go one inch closer to it. It might seem abandoned, but it most likely is not. Mother bear is probably very close, and female bears fiercely defend their young.

If you see a cub is on the trail ahead, consider abandoning your hike. If not, at least go back down the trail, take a long break, and then proceed up the trail making lots of metallic noise.

BE READY

If you brought a repellent such as pepper spray, don't bury it in your pack. Keep it as accessible as possible. Most pepper spray comes in a holster or somehow conveniently attaches to your belt or pack. Such protection won't do you any good if you can't have it ready to fire in one or two seconds. Before hitting the trail, read the directions carefully and even test fire the spray.

REGULATIONS ARE FOR YOUR SAFETY

Nobody likes rules and regulations. However, national parks and forests have a few that you must follow. These rules aren't meant to take the freedom out of your trip. They are meant to help bring you back safely.

When you get a backcountry camping permit in a national park, you get a list of these rules. In some cases, they are printed right on your permit. In national forests, you usually don't need a permit, but you can check with the local ranger for any special regulations. In both national parks and forests, take a few minutes to read the notices posted on the information board at the trailhead.

BUT I DIDN'T SEE ANY BEARS!

Now you know how to be safe. Walk up the trail constantly clanging two metal pans together. It works every time. You won't see a bear, but you'll hate your "wilderness experience." You left the city to get away from loud noise.

Yes, you can be very, very safe, but how safe do you want to be and still be able to enjoy your trip? It's a balancing act. First, be knowledgeable and then decide how far you want to go. Everybody has to make his or her own personal choice.

Here's another conflict. If you do everything recommended in this book, you most likely will not see any bears—or any deer or moose or eagles or any other wildlife. Again, you make the choice. If you want to be as safe as possible, follow these rules religiously. If you want to see wildlife, including bears, do all of this in reverse, but then, you are increasing your chances of an encounter instead of decreasing it.

HIKING

The Bear Essentials

Knowledge is the best defense.

There is no substitute for alertness.

Hike with a large group and stay together.

Don't hike alone in bear country.

Stay on the trail.

Hike in the middle of the day.

Make metallic noise.

Never approach a bear.

Cubs are deadly.

Stay away from carcasses.

Defensive hiking works. Try it.

4

Camping in Bear Country

Already our studies were revealing that the grizzly did not fear man but preferred to avoid him when possible and, as other bear-man confrontations showed, to combat him if necessary.—Dr. Frank C. Craighead, Jr.

Staying overnight in bear country is not dangerous, but it adds a slight additional risk to your trip. The main differences are the presence of more food, cooking, and garbage. Plus, you are in bear country at a time when bears are usually most active. Once again, however, following a few basic rules greatly minimizes this risk.

GET A PERMIT

Most national parks require backpackers to have a backcountry camping permit. One reason for this system is safety. If a bear has been raiding camps in one area in the park, rangers probably won't allow any overnight camping there.

The backcountry campsite reservation system also provides an opportunity to discuss the bear situation with a knowledgeable ranger. After you select a campsite, ask the ranger about bear activity in the area. In some cases, you can get brochures or watch a short video on camping in bear country.

Most national forests don't have designated campsites, but it's still wise to stop in at the local ranger station and ask about bear activity before heading for the trailhead.

SELECTING A CAMPSITE

Choosing a safe campsite is crucial. Bears and people sometimes like the same places, so don't take this decision lightly.

Sometimes, you have little to say about where you camp. If you're backpacking in a national park, regulations probably require that you stay in a precisely located campsite reserved in advance.

Fortunately, the National Park Service carefully considers the bear situation before designating campsites, and you do have a choice of which designated campsite you reserve. Discussing the bear situation with the ranger might prompt you to choose one site over another.

In most national forests, you can camp anywhere. Forest Service regulations might require you to camp certain distances from water or trails, but you aren't confined to a specific campsite.

WHEN YOU GET THERE

When you get to your chosen campsite, immediately think about bears. Look around for bear sign. If you see fresh sign, move on to another site with no signs of bear activity. If you see a bear in or near the campsite, don't camp there—even if you're in a national park and you have reserved this campsite. If you have time before nightfall, return to the trailhead and report the incident to a ranger. If it's getting late, you have little choice but to camp at an undesignated site and report it to the ranger after you finish the hike. Don't get yourself in a situation where you have to hike or set up camp in the dark.

Being careful not to camp in a campsite frequented by bears is perhaps the most important precaution you can take. Unfortunately, people who cause a bear to become conditioned to human food or garbage are rarely the people who get injured by that bear. The person who is injured usually comes along later and unknowingly camps in the same site where a bear has become accustomed to getting human food.

Look for signs of previous campers. If you see food scraps, litter, and other signs that the previous campers might not have used safe bear-country camping techniques, you might want to choose another campsite.

This is a good reason to plan your hike so you don't have to set up camp right at nightfall, which doesn't leave time to move to another campsite. If you're setting up camp in the dark, you have little chance to check around for bear sign or signs of previous campers.

KEY FEATURES OF A GOOD CAMPSITE

One key feature of a good campsite in bear country is a place to store food. Most designated sites in national parks and some national forests have a food storage device or "bear pole." (When hiking in national forests, check with the local district ranger offices for a list of campsites with bear poles.) However, in most national forests and in some national parks, you're on your own, so scout the campsite for trees that can double as a food storage device. You need a tree at least 100 yards from your tent with a large branch or two trees close enough to suspend your food between them on a rope. You can also use a tree that has partially fallen and is still leaning securely on other trees. In any case, however, the trees must be tall enough to get the food at least 10 feet off the ground and 4 feet from the tree trunk.

Choose a campsite away from popular fishing areas such as along spawning streams or the inlet of a lake. If previous campers fished in close proximity to camp, they may have left dead fish or fish entrails around camp. The smell of fish definitely attracts bears.

Avoid camping along trails, streams, or lakeshores, which often serve as travel corridors for bears. Since bears like to travel and remain concealed in trees, camp in an open area. But if you do camp in a forest, look for a campsite with large climbable trees (just in case!), and then position your tent so this "escape tree" is close to the front door.

One of the worst possible campsites is along

the trail in thick brush or timber. Because thick vegetation makes travel more difficult for all animals, bears will likely use the trail as the path of least resistance and pass dangerously close to you during the night.

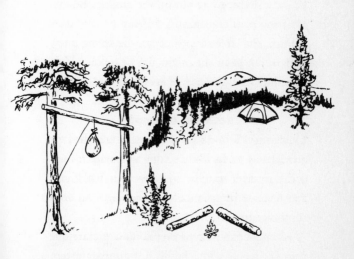

A safe campsite for camping in bear country.

FREE SLEEPING INVITES DISASTER

One particularly bad habit in national parks is often called "free sleeping." In an attempt to save money or when all the campgrounds are full, park visitors might pull off the road in an undesignated camping area and pitch a tent or, even worse, just throw a sleeping bag out on the ground. Besides violating park regulations, this can be very dangerous. The "free sleeper" might be saving a few dollars, but he or she might also be unknowingly camping in an area heavily used by bears.

SETTING UP CAMP

Once you've found a good campsite, take the next crucial step of correctly setting up camp. It's not as simple as it sounds. Some camping traditions can increase the chance of a bear entering your camping area.

You probably have seen photos of picturesque camping scenes with a family just outside the tent entrance sitting around the fire cooking dinner.

Forget this. The sleeping area and the cooking area must be separated by at least 100 yards.

Try to set up the tent at least 100 yards upwind from the cooking area. Also, if possible, pitch the tent uphill from the cooking area. Since night breezes in the mountains usually blow downhill, the wind carries food smells away from the sleeping area instead of over it.

This might create some extra walking and inconvenience, but in the unusual circumstance where a bear does come into camp, it's likely to go straight for the smell of food. In other words, it's likely to go where you have been cooking and eating. You don't want to be sleeping there. Concentrate all food smells in the cooking area and keep them away from your sleeping area.

Park rangers encourage backpackers to hang food as close to the cooking area as possible, and in many designated campsites in national parks, the "food pole" has been erected beside the designated cooking area. This concentrates all food smells in one area.

Experienced backpackers have gotten in the habit of conveniently separating all cooking area items from all sleeping area items in the pack. Then, while setting up camp, they routinely and conveniently separate them into two piles.

No-trace camping equals safe bear-country camping.

NOT UNDER THE STARS

Some people prefer to sleep out under the stars instead of using a tent. This might be okay in areas not frequented by bears, but it's not a good idea in bear country. The thin fabric of a tent certainly isn't any real physical protection from a bear, but it does present a psychological barrier to a bear who wants to come even closer.

STORING FOOD AND GARBAGE

If the campsite doesn't have an established food storage device, be sure to set one up or at least locate one before it gets dark. It's not only difficult to store food after darkness falls, but it's easier to forget some juicy morsel on the ground. Also, be sure to store food in airtight, waterproof bags to prevent food odors from circulating throughout the forest. For double protection, put food and garbage in zip-locked bags and then seal tightly in a larger plastic bag.

The following illustrations depict three popular methods. In any case, try to get food and garbage at least 10 feet off the ground.

Always try to keep food odors off your pack, but if you fail, put the food bag inside and hang the pack.

Store food at least 100 yards from the tent. You can store it near the cooking area to further concentrate food smells.

Hanging food and garbage between two trees

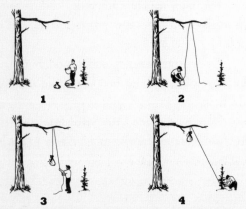

Hanging food and garbage over a tree branch

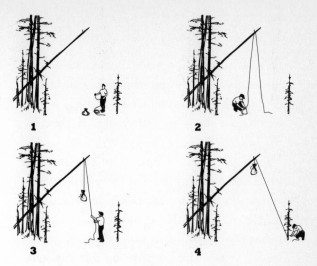

Hanging food and garbage over a leaning tree

SPECIAL EQUIPMENT

It's not really a piece of equipment, but one item you definitely need is a good supply of zip-locked bags. This handy invention is perfect for keeping food smell to a minimum and helps keep food from spilling on your pack, clothing, or other gear.

Take a special bag for storing food. The bag

must be sturdy and waterproof. You can get dry bags at most outdoor specialty stores, but you can get by with a trash compactor bag. Regular garbage bags can break and leave your food spread on the ground.

There are several varieties of bear-resistant containers on the market, but they add unwanted weight to a pack. You can check out some of the new lighter models, but in most cases, an airtight plastic bag will suffice. However, check local regulations. A few national parks are contemplating requiring bear-resistant food storage containers in alpine areas.

You also need 100 feet of nylon cord. You don't need a heavy climbing rope to store food. Go light instead. Parachute cord will usually suffice unless you plan to hang large quantities of food and gear (which might be the case on a long backpacking excursion with a large group).

You can also buy a small pulley system to make hoisting a heavy load easier. Again, you can usually get by without this extra weight in your pack unless you have a massive load to hang.

GETTING THE FOOD UP THERE

People get hurt hanging their food at night, so be careful.

The classic method is tying a rock or piece of wood to the end of your rope and tossing it over the branch and then attaching the rope to the bag or backpack and hoisting it up 10 feet or more. If the load gets too heavy, wrap it around a small tree or branch for leverage.

Use gloves so you don't get rope burns. And, of course, don't let the rock or wood come down on your head (it happens!). Also, don't let anybody stand under the bag until you're sure it's securely in place.

(As a footnote: be careful not to leave your rope behind the next morning. Once you've un-tied your food, slowly pull your rope over the branch. Don't jerk it. If the rope gets stuck and you can't climb the tree, you have to leave it behind.)

WHAT TO HANG

To be as safe as possible, store everything that has any food smell. This includes cooking gear, eating utensils, bags used to keep food in your pack, all garbage, and even clothes with food smells on them. If you spilled something on your clothes, change into other clothes for sleeping and hang clothes with food smells with the food and garbage. If you take them into the tent, you aren't separating your sleeping area from food smells.

WHAT TO KEEP IN YOUR TENT

You can't be too careful in keeping food smells out of the tent. Just in case a bear has become accustomed to coming into that campsite looking for food, it's vital to keep all food smells out of the tent. This often includes your pack, which is hard to keep odor-free. Usually only take valuables (such as cameras and binoculars), clothing, and sleeping gear into the tent.

If you brought a bear repellent such as pepper spray, sleep with it. Also, keep a flashlight in the tent. If an animal comes into camp and wakes you up, you need the flashlight to identify it.

CAMPING ABOVE TREELINE

Camping above treeline makes food storage difficult, so camp at lower elevations if possible. If you must camp above treeline, store the food at least 200 yards downwind and downhill from your sleeping area.

If you can find a cliff nearby, hang the food over the cliff. If you can't find a cliff, put the bag on top of a large boulder to at least get it off the ground. In areas of heavy bear activity, you can get a guaranteed waterproof bag and submerge food overnight. You can also take a bear-resistant container along for this specific purpose, but check the regulations first.

If all else fails, simply make the food bag as airtight as possible and leave it on the ground at least 200 yards from your sleeping area.

THE CAMPFIRE

Regulations prohibit campfires in many wild areas, but if you're in an area where fires are allowed, treat yourself. Besides adding to the nightly entertainment, the fire might make your camp safer from bears.

The campfire provides the best possible way to get rid of food smells. Build a small but hot fire and burn everything that smells of food—garbage, leftovers, fish entrails, everything. If you brought food in cans or other incombustible containers, burn them, too. You can even dump extra water from cooking or dish water on the edge of the fire to erase the smell.

Be very sure you have the fire hot enough to completely burn everything. If you leave partially burned food scraps in the fire, you are setting up a dangerous situation for the next camper who uses this site.

Before leaving camp the next morning, dig out the fire pit and pack out anything that has not completely burned, even if you believe it no longer carries food smells. For example, many foods like dried soup or hot chocolate come in foil packages that might seem like they burn, but they really don't. Pack out the scorched foil and cans (now with very minor food smells). Also, pack out foil and cans left by other campers.

Burning leftovers in campfires is not allowed in some national forests and national parks, so be sure to check local regulations before heading for the trailhead.

TYPES OF FOOD

Don't get paranoid about the types of food you bring. All food has some smell, and you can make your trip much less enjoyable by fretting too much over food.

Perhaps the safest option is freeze-dried food.

It carries very little smell, and it comes in convenient envelopes that allow you to "cook it" by merely adding boiling water. This means you don't have cooking pans to wash or store. However, freeze-dried food is very expensive, and many backpackers don't use it—and still safely enjoy bear country.

Dry, pre-packed meals (often pasta- or rice-based) offer an affordable compromise to freeze-dried foods. Also, take your favorite high-energy snack and don't worry about it. Avoid fresh fruit and canned meats and fish.

The key point is this. *What* food you have along is much less critical than *how* you handle it, cook it, and store it. A can of tuna fish might put out a smell, but if you eat all of it in one meal, don't spill it on the ground or your clothes, and burn the can later, it can be quite safe.

Hanging food at night is not the only storage issue. Also, make sure you place it correctly in your pack. Use airtight packages as much as possible.

Store food in the containers it came in or, when opened, in zip-locked bags. This keeps food smell out of your pack and off your other camping gear and clothes.

HOW TO COOK

The overriding philosophy of cooking in bear country is to create as little odor as possible. Keep it simple. Use as few pans and dishes as possible. And don't cook more than you can eat, so you don't have to deal with leftovers.

Unless it's a weather emergency, don't cook in the tent. If you like to winter camp, you probably cook in the tent, but you should have a different tent for summer camping.

If you can have a campfire and decide to cook fish, try cooking in aluminum foil envelopes instead of frying or roasting the fish over an open flame. Then, after removing the cooked fish, quickly burn the fish scraps off the foil. Using foil also means you don't have to wash the pan you used to cook the fish.

Be careful not to spill on yourself while cooking. If you do, change clothes and hang the clothes with food odor with the food and garbage. Wash your hands thoroughly before retiring to the tent.

LEFTOVERS

Try hard not to cook too much food, so you don't have to deal with leftovers. If you do end up with extra food, however, you only have two choices: carry it out or burn it. Don't bury it or throw it in a lake or leave it anywhere in bear country. A bear most likely will find and dig up any food or garbage buried in the backcountry.

TAKING OUT THE GARBAGE

In bear country, you have only two choices for dealing with garbage—burn it or carry it out. Since campfires are prohibited in many areas, prepare for garbage problems before you leave home. Bring along airtight zip-locked bags to store garbage. Be sure to hang your garbage at night along with your food. Also, carry in as little garbage as possible by discarding excess packaging while packing.

WASHING DISHES

This is a sticky problem, but there is one easy solution. If you don't dirty dishes, you don't have to wash them. So try to minimize food smell by using as few dishes and pans as possible. If you use the principles of no-trace camping, you are probably doing as much as you can to reduce food smell from dishes.

If you brought paper towels, use one to carefully remove food scraps from pans and dishes before washing them. Then, when you wash dishes, you will have much less food smell. Burn the dirty towels or store them in zip-locked bags with other garbage. Put pans and dishes in zip-locked bags before putting them back in your pack.

If you end up with lots of food scraps in the dish water, drain out the scraps and store them in zip-locked bags with other garbage or burn them. You can bring a lightweight screen to filter out food scraps from dish water, but be sure to store the screen with the food and garbage. If you have a campfire, pour the dish water around the edge of the fire. If you don't have a fire, take the dish water at least 100 yards downwind and downhill from camp and pour it on the ground. Don't put dish water or food scraps in a lake or stream.

Finally, don't put it off. Do dishes immediately after eating to minimize food smells.

Although possibly counter to accepted rules of cleanliness for many people, you can skip washing dishes altogether on the last night of your trip. Instead, simply use the paper towels to clean the dirty dishes as much as possible. You can wash them when you get home. Pack dirty dishes in airtight bags before putting them back in your pack.

DOG AND HORSE FOOD

It's usually unwise to take dogs into bear country,

and it's prohibited in many national parks. If you do it, treat the dog food like human food. Store it in airtight bags, and hang it at night.

Although horses don't increase your risk of encountering a bear, the large amount of food necessary for horses does pose an additional risk. Again, treat it as carefully as you do human food. Horse pellets are like little candy bars to bears.

NO SAFE SEX
Some bear experts believe that human sexual activity attracts bears. So try not to be in the mood until you get out of bear country.

CAR CAMPING
Don't have the attitude that vehicle campgrounds offer added security from bears. In some cases, the reverse might be true.

If you're sleeping in a tent, there isn't much difference between backcountry camping and camping in a vehicle campground. Be equally careful with food and garbage.

One advantage you have in a vehicle campground is food storage. Keep food and garbage in airtight containers and then store it in your car at night. Keep food smells out of the tent.

One disadvantage of vehicle campgrounds is the size of the campsite. You can't effectively separate your sleeping area from your cooking area.

Also, look around for bear sign, and if you see any, go for another campsite. If you see a culvert trap in the area, it usually means rangers are trying to remove problem bears. This is a good tip-off to go elsewhere.

DO SOMEBODY A BIG FAVOR

Report all bear sightings to the ranger after your trip. This might not help you, but it could save another camper's life. If rangers get enough reports to spot a pattern, they will manage the area accordingly and not unknowingly allow camping in a potentially hazardous situation.

CAMPING

The Bear Essentials

Choose a safe campsite.

Camp below treeline.

Separate cooking and sleeping areas.

Sleep in a tent.

Cook just the right amount of food and eat it all.

Store food and garbage out of reach of bears.

Never feed bears.

Keep food odors out of the tent.

Leave the campsite cleaner than you found it.

Leave no food rewards for bears.

Attractants and Deterrents

The answer to the oft-asked question "What attracts and deters bears?" is the same as lots of other questions about bears. The answer is: Nobody really knows.

EVERYBODY HAS A THEORY

Amateurs and professionals alike have theories on what might attract or deter bears. Some say strong unnatural smells from cosmetics, perfume, or scented soap attract bears. Others say the opposite —that these smells keep bears away. Bright colors might attract bears, but they might also deter them. The same goes for unusual sounds.

There are lots of suspects—new fabrics used in backpacking equipment, chemicals used to waterproof tents or coats, white gas used in stoves, campfire smoke. The list goes on and on, but nobody knows.

GARBAGE BRINGS THEM IN

Actually, you already know that the smell of human food and garbage brings in bears. So if you don't want to attract bears, be extremely careful not to disperse food smells.

AVOID STRONG SMELLS

Experts agree on at least two things: bears have a supersensitive sense of smell, and they tend to be curious. Given these two facts, it seems best to avoid any strong scents that might excite a bear's curiosity. Concentrate on smelling like a good ol' sweaty human being who needs a shower.

MOTHBALLS

Old timers used to spread mothballs around the perimeter of their camp under the theory that bears hated this smell and wouldn't cross the mothball barrier. In recent times, ammonia has been used in the same manner. In both cases, however, there is no scientific evidence to say that it works. If you spread mothballs, collect them all in the morning and pack them out. You don't want to leave unsightly and smelly litter in the campsite.

RESEARCH HOLDS PROMISE

In answering this question, research has lots to offer. If scientists could come up with an environmentally sensitive chemical, sound, or color to keep bears out of campsites, it could create a collective sigh of relief from legions of backpackers.

DON'T TAKE CHANCES

In the meantime, don't take chances. Avoid unusual sounds or strong smells. Use natural colors. Be "normal." Obviously, backpackers aren't commonly using anything that actively attracts bears. Otherwise, there would be many more encounters. As long as you use the same type of equipment and food normally used by backpackers, you're likely to be safe.

6

For Your Protection

Protecting yourself is the second priority. The first priority is preventing a situation where you have to protect yourself or use a repellent.

GUNS

Traditionally, travelers in bear country carried firearms, and in the hands of a skilled person, guns can offer the desired level of protection. Regrettably, the aftermath of this success is a dead bear.

In unskilled hands, however, guns can make the situation worse. A misplaced shot can wound and infuriate a bear. A heavy caliber is required to down a grizzly bear. This makes gun-handling experience even more critical. If you decide to take a gun, go to a gun expert and get good advice on what type of firearm to take. Then, before you go, get lots of practice.

Keep in mind that guns are only an option in national forests. All national parks prohibit carrying firearms on backcountry trails.

LOUD NOISE

Guns can be used as noise-makers to scare off bears. The same goes for loudly banging pans together, firecrackers, air horns, and other loud noise. Loud noise is more likely to work with black bears than grizzlies.

MILD AGGRESSION

If a black bear comes into camp, use mild aggression to scare it off. Run toward the bear, throwing things, and yelling or making other loud noises. Don't get too close, and be sure you don't accidentally run between a female and her cubs. Also, the closer the bear gets to a food reward, the harder it will be to scare the bear off. So don't wait until the bear gets too close to show it who is boss.

Mild aggression will usually run off a black bear. However, don't use this option with grizzlies. It may result in a counterattack.

PEPPER SPRAY

In recent years, pepper spray has earned more and more respect from bear experts. More than 60 people have escaped encounters uninjured by turning away a charging bear with pepper spray. Now, most park rangers carry it when in bear country.

In no recorded case did it make a bear more aggressive or harm the bear. In fact, one could argue that getting sprayed with pepper spray helps the bear by making it more wary of humans. This "adverse conditioning," as bear experts call it, will also make the area safer for the next hiker.

Before you leave the trailhead, read the directions. Test fire the spray–but not into the wind. It will drift back and give you the personal experience of what a bear feels like when sprayed.

Also, make sure you carry it in a readily accessible place. You can buy a handy holster at most sports stores. And remember the limited range of the spray, usually from 15 to 30 feet.

Pepper spray is not a cure-all. It's merely your next-to-last line of defense. If it doesn't turn away the bear, your only remaining option is playing dead.

Even though pepper spray can help erase that deep-seated fear that can ruin a trip to bear country, it has a downside. Pepper spray can create a false sense of security. Pepper spray doesn't make you totally safe. That's why bear experts say, "It's not brains in cans."

Even with pepper spray conveniently mounted on your belt, you must follow all other precautions outlined in Chapters 3 and 4. Poor handling of food and garbage can get you (or other campers who follow you) into much more trouble with bears than pepper spray can solve. Pepper spray does not make you bear-proof.

HOW TO USE PEPPER SPRAY

The inventor and major supplier of pepper spray (and the only spray to be scientifically tested), Counter Assault, distributes the following recommendations for use of the spray during an encounter.

1. If the bear approaches within 30 feet, give it a warning blast, placing a cloud of spray between you and the bear.

2. If the bear continues to approach or charge within 20 feet, give it one or two more blasts, aiming at the face.

3. If the bear approaches within 10 feet, give it a 4- or 5-second continuous blast, aiming directly into the bear's face and eyes. Continue to fire until the bear retreats or until the canister is exhausted.

4. If the bear makes contact with you, play dead.

(As a footnote: some airlines have special regulations about carrying pepper spray, and you will have trouble getting it across the Canada/USA border. Also, be careful when storing it, since you can't let it get too hot or too cold.)

7

Close
Encounters

The thing that makes me very unhappy about the whole incident is my fear that this will only add fuel to the fire for those people who advocate the destruction of the grizzly to make our national parks safe. There is no reason, in the name of civilized progress, to kill an animal for doing what is natural.

I feel no malice toward the bear. It was my fault for sticking my neck out too far. The bear was only protecting her young and her territory.

The only thing that will prevent me from hiking in the wilderness again is the eventual destruction of the wilderness itself, and when anyone advocates the destruction of grizzlies, he is in essence advocating the destruction of the true wilderness. Let us pray that this never happens.—ROBERT HAHM, 1968 MAULING VICTIM.

Having a close encounter with a bear is like having a heart attack. If you practice preventive health care, stay physically fit, and watch your diet, you probably won't have heart problems. Likewise, if you follow the safety measures in this book, you probably won't have bear problems. Preventing an encounter is, by far, the priority.

WHAT IS AN ENCOUNTER?

A bear sighting (seeing a bear at a safe distance) is not an encounter. An encounter is a situation where you may be at risk. It's what happens when hikers or campers don't follow all the recommendations listed earlier in this book.

An encounter could be surprising a bear on or

near the trail. It could be a bear coming into camp. But all encounters have one common characteristic: great care must be taken to avoid injury.

DISAGREEMENT ABOUNDS

If you're uncertain about what to do in case of an encounter, you're not alone. Even bear experts disagree on how to react to various kinds of encounters. Consequently, there is no checklist on what to do.

Everybody does agree, however, that every encounter is different, and every bear is different—and that the actions you take during the encounter can definitely affect your chances of coming away uninjured.

HAVE A DRESS REHEARSAL

Not many recommendations apply to all encounters, but one does—cool heads prevail. Panic is your greatest enemy.

Rehearse. Go through hypothetical situations

and decide what each member of the group would do. This is a vital part of your preparation for your trip to bear country. It builds self-confidence throughout the group, and you can head into the wilderness knowing how you would react to an encounter with a bear.

IF YOU SEE A BEAR AT A DISTANCE

Take a moment to enjoy this rare and beautiful sight. Then, take a big detour around the bear, upwind if possible, so the bear can get your scent. Stay out of sight, if possible, and make metallic noise to make sure the bear knows you are there. Then, quickly leave the area, but don't run.

IF YOU SEE A BEAR
ON OR NEAR THE TRAIL

Stand your ground and put your hand on the pepper spray. If possible, take a wide, upwind detour. If terrain prevents a detour, back down the trail for several hundred yards. Take a short break, and then, come back up the trail making lots of metallic noise. The bear should be out of sight when you get back to your original vantage point.

If the bear is still there, abandon your trip. If the bear is between you and the trailhead, you should go a mile or so back up the trail and wait several hours before trying to get out to your vehicle.

IF YOU SEE A BEAR AT CLOSE RANGE

Most important, don't panic or run wildly or scream. Running or other sudden movements might cause the bear to charge.

The first thing to do is nothing—make no sudden moves or sounds. Stand still. Be quiet. Get your pepper spray ready to go. Then, take a few seconds to carefully assess the situation.

Try to identify the bear as a black bear or grizzly. Both are dangerous, but grizzlies are usually more ill-tempered.

Keep your backpack on. Look around for cubs.

Scout around for climbable trees. And then plot your next move. As long as you stay cool-headed and under control, you have an excellent chance of leaving this encounter with only vivid memories, not injuries.

Also, try to determine if the bear is merely curious or truly aggressive. Watch for aggressive behavior, such as laid-back ears, hackles up on the back of its neck, head rapidly swinging from side to side, threatening "woofs," or feet slapping on the ground. If the bear mashes its teeth together making a loud "pop," it's very agitated and likely to charge.

If the bear stands on its hind feet and puts its snout up, it's not a sign of aggression. The bear is trying to get your scent or get a better look at you.

Aggressive behavior is your cue that the bear is probably warning you to get out of its turf. You should oblige.

Any bear that moves toward you should be considered aggressive. Drop something like a fanny pack, extra clothing, camera, or water bottle to distract and delay the bear. Don't drop anything with food in it. You don't want to give the bear a food reward for chasing you.

If you decide to go for the tree you spotted, make sure you can reach the tree and get 15 feet up the tree before the bear gets there. Running toward the tree could easily prompt the bear to run after you. Remember, bears can sprint at 40 mph. Hikers who underestimated a bear's speed have been mauled trying to get up trees.

It's usually best to back away slowly, talking quietly in a monotone voice. Avoid sudden movements. Don't turn your back on the bear. Don't kneel down. Act non-threatening and submissive. Avoid direct eye contact with the bear. Slowly move your arms up and down (like doing jumping jacks without jumping) as you retreat.

IF YOU SEE A BEAR CHARGING YOU

It's easy to say and hard to do, but again, don't

panic. Many charges are actually bluff charges. Get your pepper spray ready to fire and stand your ground. Sometimes, a bear will make several bluff charges. Don't use the pepper spray unless you're sure the bear is not bluffing and is within range of the spray.

If the bear stops after a bluff charge, slowly wave your arms, talk softly, and slowly back away.

If the bear doesn't stop, use the pepper spray. If that doesn't work, play dead. This tells the bear you are not a threat.

Curl up in the cannonball position on your stomach, knees against your chest and hands clasped over the back of your neck. Remain silent. Leave your pack on to shield your body. If the bear roughs you up a bit, don't fight back, and stay in your tuck. If the bear swats you, stay curled up. Don't look at the bear. If the bear moves away, continue to play dead for few minutes, then cautiously look around to make sure the bear is gone. If so, quickly (no running!) move out of the area. If the bear is still nearby, hold your position and remain silent.

Playing dead. If you're wearing a backpack, leave it on.

If the bear continues to maul you while you are playing dead, give up the game and use whatever physical resistance you can muster as a last resort. If you see one of your hiking partners in this situation, intervene on his or her behalf.

(As a footnote: most bear experts believe in

playing dead, but some experts also believe that playing dead does not work with black bears. If you have positively identified the bear as a black bear, you might try using whatever physical resistance you can to fight the bear off. However, if you aren't sure of the identification, play dead.)

IF YOU SEE A BEAR FROM YOUR CAMP

If the bear is at a distance, get the pepper spray out and make lots of metallic noise to scare it away. Then, if there is still time before nightfall, break camp and move to another campsite. Seeing a bear during the day from a camp might mean that the bear will come into the camp at night.

If the bear is close to camp, move to the base of the escape trees you previously scouted out. Take noise-makers and pepper spray with you. If you have time, take the food, too, so the bear doesn't get a food reward. If the bear comes closer, get up the tree. If you don't have trees or time to get up them, stand together with the pepper spray ready and use it if the bear comes dangerously close and within range.

IF A BEAR COMES INTO CAMP
DURING DAYLIGHT

A bear coming into camp is not the same bear you surprise on the trail. This bear has chosen to approach you. It's probably a bear that has become conditioned to human food and garbage, and it might be looking for its next meal. This bear is much more dangerous because it has stopped trying to avoid an encounter.

The bear might not intend to attack. More likely, it's looking for a food reward. Try to prevent the bear from getting it. Allowing the bear to get more food only makes it even more dangerous for you and the next camper.

Stay calm. Avoid direct eye contact. Talk softly, and slowly retreat. If you have to abandon the camp and sacrifice your camping gear, do it. Return to the trailhead and immediately report the encounter.

If the bear moves toward you, react in the same way you would if you met the bear on the trail.

IF A BEAR COMES
INTO YOUR CAMP AT NIGHT

Get the pepper spray ready, and then, look out of the tent and check out the bear with your flashlight. First, you should verify that it's a bear. It might be a campground deer or one of your hiking partners who can't sleep.

If it's a black bear after a free meal, the situation is usually not as serious as a grizzly coming into camp. If you have time to get to your escape tree, do it, but don't leave the tent if you aren't sure you have time. If the bear (black or grizzly) is hanging around the cooking area because of the food smell, make lots of noise and try to scare the bear away.

IF A BEAR COMES INTO YOUR TENT

This is the worst possible situation. It very rarely

happens, but there are a few documented cases.

A night attack usually comes from a predatory bear. If you act like prey, you become prey.

Once more, don't panic, run, or scream, but don't remain calm. Instead, fight back with everything you have. Don't lie still in your sleeping bag. Don't play dead. Use the pepper spray. Make loud metallic noise. Use the air horn. Shine lights in the bear's eyes. Temporarily blind the bear with the flash on your camera. Use any repellent you brought with you. Unload on the bear with everything you have. Anything goes. Use whatever physical resistance you can.

GENERALIZATIONS MAY BE MORE DANGEROUS THAN BEARS

The above recommendations have been boiled down from personal experience, extensive research through written literature, and many discussions with bear experts. But these are only general guidelines. They won't work every time. Special situations and special bears won't fit guidelines.

One thing is clear: stay calm and try to ration-
ally evaluate the situation. If you have studied up
on bears and if your group has had dress rehearsals,
you can, in most cases, safely survive an encounter.

BE REALISTIC

After reading a few pages about how to deal with
encounters, it's difficult to overcome the fear of
bears. But be realistic. If you practice the methods
outlined in Chapters 3 and 4, you have only the
slightest chance of ever having an encounter. And
even if you do, you stand a good chance of coming out of it unscathed.

If bears wanted to prey on humans, it would
be easy. Bears could easily kill hundreds of people
every year. Obviously 99.9 percent of the bears (or
more) only want to be separated from people. Keep
this in mind as you prepare for—and then enjoy—
your trip to bear country.

THE ENCOUNTER

The Bear Essentials

Preventing an encounter is the highest priority.

Have a dress rehearsal.

Be prepared. Bring pepper spray.

There is no checklist on what to do.

Remember every encounter is different.

Cool heads prevail. Panic is your greatest enemy.

Carefully assess each situation.

Don't run. Talk softly and slowly retreat.

A bear coming into camp is much more dangerous.

A night attack comes from a predatory bear.

If you act like prey, you become prey.

Keep the risk of an encounter in perspective.

Special Precautions for Women

Most bear-country hiking and camping techniques apply equally to men and women. However, women should take a few extra precautions.

NO SMELL IS THE BEST SMELL

As recommended earlier in this book, you should avoid strong smells when in bear country. This goes for men and women. However, many feminine products, in particular, are heavily scented. Avoid these strong odors, since they might attract bears. Search for unscented products, or even better, go without. You probably do not need cosmetics, lotion, or perfume in the wilderness, but if you can't go without, work hard to keep the odor to a minimum.

MENSTRUATION

Bear experts disagree on the safety of women traveling in bear country during their menstrual periods. Some authorities recommend women stay out of bear country during menstrual periods, but others believe this is an overreaction.

Field tests under controlled conditions have shown that bears are attracted to menstrual odor and several other strong odors. To date, however, there is no evidence that bears are attracted to menstrual odor more than any other odor. In addition, no known bear attack has been traced to menstruation as a cause. Nonetheless, common sense dictates that since bears have a keen sense of smell, women should take extra precautions during menstruation.

Keep yourself as clean and odor free as possible. Use pre-moistened, unscented cleaning towelettes, and use tampons instead of pads.

Never bury used tampons or towelettes. A bear could easily smell them and dig up this little "reward." This could endanger the next woman to come down the trail.

Place all used tampons and towelettes in double zip-locked bags and store them with other garbage in a bear-resistant container or hang them 10 feet off the ground.

If you have a campfire, burn tampons and towelettes. Make sure the fire is hot and burns long enough to completely consume them. Before you leave camp, dig any unburned, charred remains out of the fire pit and pack them with other garbage.

Nobody knows the answer to the basic question, "Should women go into bear country during their menstrual period?" An equally important—and unanswered—question is, "Does menstrual odor serve as a deterrent or an attractant?" Menstrual odor could attract bears into camp, but this strong "human scent" could deter bears from coming near camp.

MAKING THE CHOICE

There is no scientific evidence indicating that women are at a greater risk during menstrual periods than they are at any other time. If you choose to go into bear country, take all special precautions as outlined above and elsewhere in this book, and enjoy the trip.

Special Precautions for Hunters, Anglers, and Outfitters

This book outlines the steps you can take to make your trip to bear country as safe as possible, but if you wanted to make the trip as hazardous as possible, you would employ many techniques commonly used by hunters and anglers. Hunters want to surprise wildlife, and they work hard at being as quiet as possible. The same goes for anglers stalking a big trout in a mountain stream. Consequently, hunters and anglers must make a difficult compromise between safety and success.

In reality, hunting (especially big game hunting) will, under any circumstances, be more dangerous than hiking. Hunters silently stalk around the woods during early morning and late evening. In many cases, they will quietly walk through bear country in darkness to reach a good vantage point at first light. Some bear experts are starting to believe that bears might even be attracted by gunfire which could be associated with the presence of fresh meat or a gut pile.

FOR HUNTERS AND OUTFITTERS

Even though there is a limit to what hunters can do and still hope for any chance of success, they should consider these extra precautions:

- When hiking to a favorite spot during darkness, use a flashlight.
- When camping out, select and set up the camp as described in Chapter 4.
- Don't hunt alone.
- Make extra noise when driving game out of thick

brush or dense thickets of small trees.

- If you see a carcass or gut pile left by another hunter, don't go near it.
- If a big game hunt is successful, field dress the animal as quickly as possible.
- Quickly separate the carcass from the gut pile. Use a sheet of heavy plastic to move the gut pile about 100 yards from the carcass.
- Don't leave your gut pile near a trail or campsite where a bear might claim it and create circumstances that could threaten other hunters or hikers using the trail or campsite.
- Don't drag a carcass into camp. A bear might follow the scent trail.
- If you leave a carcass unattended, hang it 10 feet off the ground just like backpackers hang their food and garbage at night. If necessary, cut the meat into smaller pieces to facilitate hanging. (Required in some national forests.)
- Hang any carcasses at least 100 yards from any campsite or trail as required in some national forests. If it's not possible to hang the carcass, be sure to cache it at least 100 yards from camp.

- If you can't hang the carcass, leave it on the ground in an open area where you can observe it from a safe distance when you return to claim your prize.

- Leave an article of clothing (ripe with human scent) on or near the carcass or pour ammonia around the carcass to deter bears.

- Noisily return to the carcass upwind, so the bear can get your scent before you get there. Thoroughly scan the area with binoculars before approaching the carcass. If you see that the carcass has been moved or partially buried, a bear may have claimed it. If a bear claims the carcass, abandon it and leave the area immediately. Do not attempt to shoot or harass the bear.

- Use horses to decrease the chance of a bear encounter.

- Watch for signs of bear activity and know bear habitat. For example, during the fall, bears are likely to be found in berry patches or in high-altitude whitebark pine stands eating pine nuts.

- When bugling for elk, be alert. Bugling not only attracts elk, but in a few cases, bears, too.

FOR ANGLERS

Anglers can also make their trip safer with a few extra precautions:

- Remember that bears like to travel along streams and lakeshores, so when following a loud, rushing mountain stream in thick brush, make lots of noise, preferably metallic noise like an aluminum rod case clanging on rocks.

- Catch-and-release fishing is much less likely to attract a bear than having fish for dinner. Seriously consider not keeping and eating fish in bear country if you can't have a hot campfire to burn entrails and leftovers.

- Don't bury fish entrails. Burn them or pack them out. When fishing in large streams or deep lakes, you can clean the fish right where you catch them (instead of back at camp) and, after puncturing the air bladder, throw entrails into the deep water. Never leave entrails along lakeshores or in small streams.

- If you want fish for dinner, keep those you catch in the water as long as possible to keep the smell to a minimum.

- Don't clean fish anywhere near camp.
- Avoid getting fish odors on your clothes, and wash hands thoroughly after cleaning fish.

10

Special Precautions for Mountain Bikers

In recent years, mountain biking has become quite popular, including long excursions, sometimes with overnight stays, into bear country. In most national parks, the National Park Service only allows mountain biking on designated roads. In the national forests, the U.S. Forest Service prohibits mountain biking in designated wilderness areas, but allows bicycles on most other trails and roads.

Mountain bikers should, of course, carefully follow all precautions followed by backpackers, but they can take a few extra precautions to make their trip even safer.

NOISE IS EVEN MORE IMPORTANT

Mountain bikers coasting down a hill can build up some major speed, and in most cases, do not make much noise. This creates a hazardous situation because the speed and relative silence of biking will not alert a bear around a blind corner or small hill. This sets up the circumstances for a sudden encounter. The same hazardous situation could be created while cranking up a long hill and concentrating energy on getting to the top instead of looking around or making noise.

Human voices probably won't be loud enough, so rely on metallic noise. Attach a bear bell to your saddle or handlebar. The bell will constantly clang as you ride down a bumpy trail. This will be distracting but safe. You can also buy hand-operated bells for handlebars, which you can ring whenever your visibility is impaired such as on a long downhill with blind curves.

11

Special Precautions for Photographers

Trying to get a good picture of a bear, especially of a grizzly, is always risky, and photographers have been mauled and killed on failed attempts to do so. Nonetheless, photographers will rarely pass up the chance to get a good bear photo. A few guidelines might make the photo attempt safer:

• Use at least a 500 mm telephoto lens.
• Avoid direct eye contact with the bear, which could be interpreted as an act of aggression.
• Don't make unusual sounds or throw anything at the bear to prompt it into a better pose.
• If the bear moves away, don't follow or chase it.
• Maintain a distance of 1,000 feet or more. But

remember that under some circumstances, this can still be dangerous.

- Immediately retreat at any sign of the bear becoming aggressive, but don't panic and run.
- Be particularly cautious when photographing a female with cubs.
- If possible, photograph from your vehicle.
- In the backcountry, try to set up near a climbable tree tall enough to get you 10 feet off the ground.
- Never approach or try to sneak up on a bear.
- Never feed or leave food in an attempt to attract a bear. This is not only unethical but also dangerous for the photographer and for other people who might come into the area at a later date.

Living in Bear Country

We clearly have demonstrated our ability to eliminate the grizzly. Today, we are faced with a task more difficult: to co-exist with it.

— Dr. Stephen Herrero

More and more people are moving into bear country. Hardly a day goes by without news of a new resort or mine, most with accompanying residential developments for workers. Second homes and wilderness cabins regularly sprout up in many privately owned meadows in bear country. In short, more and more people are living with bears with more and more chance of conflict with bears.

If bears, and particularly grizzly bears, are to survive this forced coexistence, the residents of bear country must consider the impact of their daily activities on bears as well as their own safety.

YOUR GARBAGE COULD KILL ME

A "garbage bear" is a soon-to-be-dead bear, and somebody might get hurt along the way. If you live in bear country, you must be extremely careful not to let bears get human food or garbage. You don't want to be responsible for a regrettable chain of events that could kill somebody.

Garbage is like candy to a bear. Human food and garbage have extremely high nutritional value to bears. Before long, the "garbage bear" prefers human food over natural food. The bear becomes conditioned to garbage and will go to extremes to get it. The bear will return again and again looking for more garbage. If it can't get a food reward at your place, it will go to your neighbor's place. The bear might even abandon its normal wariness of humankind and come dangerously close to people to get food or garbage. It will climb over fences, break into cabins, or rip open dumpsters.

Sooner or later, the "problem bear" has to be killed. But before this happens, it might injure a child playing in a backyard or a hiker on a nearby trail. If it can't get human food from cabins, it might try getting some out of a backpacker's tent.

STORING GARBAGE

If you use outside garbage cans, don't put food items into them. Use outside garbage cans for non-food items only. Better yet, keep garbage in the barn, garage, or basement, completely unavailable to bears. Try to store it in a manner that even prevents odors from getting to bears.

Many communities have bear-proof dumpsters, incinerators, or other approved disposal facilities. If you decide to live in bear country, take the extra time needed to haul your garbage to these facilities.

WATCH THE KIDS

Closely supervise children. They're little and help-less and might look like easy prey to bears (even more so to mountain lions). Don't allow kids to hike out of sight without adult supervision. You might be super-conscious about not creating bear-human conflicts, but who knows what your neighbors have been doing? Even if you haven't had bears visiting your place, there still could be a "garbage bear" in the area.

PETS AND LIVESTOCK

Use the same level of caution for pet food and feed for livestock as you do for human food and gar-bage. Bears love horse pellets and dog food, but don't let them get it. When you feed livestock, try not to spill pellets, oats, or other food on the ground.

HONEY BEARS

No surprise. Bears love honey. They also love the

larval form of bees. If you live in bear country and have beehives, you will probably have bear problems. Make the hives inaccessible to bears. One common method is putting them on platforms at least 10 feet off the ground. Use metal poles or cover the wooden support poles with tin to prevent bears from climbing up for their honey treat. You can also use electric fencing to fend off bears.

FRUITS AND VEGETABLES

Fruit trees and vegetable gardens attract bears like magnets, and it's almost impossible to keep them away, especially on years when natural foods, such as huckleberries and whitebark pine nuts, have a bad crop. If you live in bear country, you really should not plant fruit trees. In addition to creating a hazardous situation for you, your family, and your neighbors, bears that become overly bold in raiding fruit trees are usually killed.

If you do have fruit trees, the best defense against bears is electric fencing. Also, try to pick all the fruit immediately after it ripens to cut down the amount of time it tempts bears. Ditto for vegetable gardens.

COMPOSTING CONFLICT

Many residents of remote areas like to use composting to cut down the amount of refuse they create. That's generally sound environmental advice, but in bear country, the odor of decomposing food in compost heaps can lure bears dangerously close to human habitations. If you live in bear country, you should not compost refuse.

BIRD FEEDERS OR BEAR FEEDERS?

Bird feeders, particularly if you use suet, can also attract bears. Only use suet in winter months when bears are having their winter sleep. Hang hummingbird feeders out of reach of bears.

THE RISK FACTORS

Many people think staying close to residential

communities is safer than hiking 10 miles into the wilderness. This may not be true.

More people always means more garbage, and if somebody hasn't used proper disposal, there could be a dangerous bear hanging around a developed area.

Conversely, most serious hikers now use no-trace camping techniques and are very careful not to let bears get human food or garbage. This could make a remote campsite safer than a backyard picnic.

LIVING IN BEAR COUNTRY

The Bear Essentials

Make sure bears don't get human food or garbage, and keep all food odors away from bears.

Never feed bears.

Bird, pet, and livestock food, beehives, and compost piles attract bears.

Don't feel extra-safe when hiking close to home.

Closely supervise children.

The Parks Are Not Enough

We should preserve grizzly bear populations, not because their ecological function is critical, but because of what they can do for human imagination, thought and experience.

—DR. STEPHEN HERRERO

I'm a lucky guy. I spend several weeks every year in bear country, and I've seen wild grizzly bears. I also spend hours reliving those magnificent moments.

Anybody who sees a grizzly in a wild setting will never forget it. I would argue that this is the best thing you can see. Viewing a grizzly in a zoo might be enjoyable and help with identification, but it's a far cry from watching a female grizzly shepherd her cubs across a rushing mountain stream.

I have taken my children into the heart of the wilderness with the specific purpose of seeing a grizzly. They saw several grizzlies, and they will always carry those experiences with them. Now, they are grown, and anxious to go back to bear country on their own.

I have had one serious encounter and a few sightings that were close enough to get the adrenaline flowing. These experiences are permanently etched in my memory, and they helped prompt me to write this book.

But there is a conflict. As more and more backpackers, hunters, anglers, mountain bikers, and climbers penetrate the last remnants of the grizzly's domain, they place more and more stress on this threatened symbol of the wilderness. It will become harder and harder for the grizzly to avoid us.

However, we can all be part of the solution,

instead of part of the problem.

I have confidence that most people interested in going into the depths of western mountains want to do whatever they can to preserve the king of those mountains, the majestic grizzly bear. It almost seems like we have an obligation to know how to avoid and react to an encounter because that unfortunate meeting might result in a grizzly being killed. We should not only be concerned with our own welfare. Our carelessness can create a "problem bear" which is, of course, a sympathetic name for a soon-to-be-dead bear.

I also have confidence that anybody who gets a glimpse of a wild grizzly will be a strong supporter of wilderness from that moment on. In some cases, it might be enough just to go to where the grizzly walks and sense the presence of the most majestic of animals. Trust me, you can feel it.

The grizzly needs your help. The grizzly needs lots of room, and civilization is growing into the last blank spots on the map. The grizzly needs wild, unroaded habitat, of course, but the big bear also needs to be accepted instead of killed by local residents. The grizzly needs your vote.

The national parks are large, but they are not enough. Park boundaries are merely lines on a map drawn for political, not ecological, reasons, and the grizzly knows nothing of these boundaries.

Only those able to see the pageant of evolution can be expected to value its theater, the wilderness, or its outstanding achievement, the grizzly.—Aldo Leopold

APPENDIX

Sources of Pepper Spray

Counter Assault
P.O. Box 4721
Missoula, MT 59801
1-800-695-3394

**Universal Defense
Alternative Products**
13160 Yonder Road
Bozeman, MT 59715
1-406-763-4242

**Guardian Personal
Security Products**
21639 N. 14th Ave.
Phoenix, AZ 85027
1-602-582-2091

Sources of Bear-Resistant Containers

Decarteret Pack Equipment
30547 Mehrten Drive
Exeter, CA 93221

Garcia Machine
14097 Avenue 272
Visalia, CA 93292
1-209-732-3785

LMI Welding, Inc.
P.O. Box 772
Cut Bank, MT 59427
1-800-345-5623

Metalworks of Montana
109 North California
Missoula, MT 59801
1-406-728-5070

Teton Welding
P.O. Box 976
Choteau, MT 59422
1-406-466-2124

**Wyoming Outdoor
Industries, Inc.**
1231 13th Street
Cody, WY 82414
1-307-527-6449

Suggested Reading

Bear Attacks
by Stephen Herrero
Lyons & Burford Publishers
ISBN 0-941130-82-1

Wild Country Companion
by Will Harmon
Falcon Press Publishing Co.
ISBN 1-56044-169-0

Conservation Organizations

Center for Wildlife Information
P.O. Box 8289
Missoula, MT 59807
1-406-721-8985

Great Bear Foundation
P.O. Box 1289
Bozeman, MT 59771
1-406-586-5533
Fax: 1-406-586-6103

Greater Yellowstone Coalition
P.O. Box 1874
Bozeman, MT 59771
1-406-586-1593
Fax: 1-406-586-0851

**National Parks
and Conservation Assocation**
1776 Massachusetts Ave. NW
Washington, DC 20036
1-202-223-6722
Fax: 1-202-659-0650

Sierra Club
730 Polk Street
San Francisco, CA 94109
1-415-776-2211

The Wilderness Society
900 17th St. NW
Washington, DC 20006
1-202-853-2300

The Author

Whenever Bill Schneider isn't hiking, he wants to be.

In the late 1960s, during college, Bill worked on a trail crew in Glacier National Park. Then he spent the 1970s publishing *Montana Outdoors* magazine for the Montana Department of Fish, Wildlife & Parks and covering as many miles of trails as possible on weekends and holidays. In 1978, he wrote his first book, *Where the Grizzly Walks*.

In 1979, Bill, along with his partner to this day, Mike Sample, created Falcon Press Publishing Company and published two guidebooks the first year. Bill wrote one of them, *Hiking Montana*, which is still a popular guidebook. He has also written six more books and many magazine articles on wildlife, outdoor recreation, and environmental issues. Along the way, on a part-time basis over the span of twelve years, Bill taught classes on hiking and camping in grizzly country for The Yellowstone Institute, a nonprofit educational organization in Yellowstone National Park.

Since 1979, Bill has served as publisher of Falcon Press which is now established as a premier publisher of recreational guidebooks, with over 300 titles in print.